Clouds

by Gail Saunders-Smith

Content Consultant:
Ken Barlow, Chief Meteorologist
KARE-TV, Minneapolis
Member, American Meteorological Society

Pebble Books
an imprint of Capstone Press

Pebble Books are published by Capstone Press,
1710 Roe Crest Drive, North Mankato, Minnesota 56003.
www.capstonepub.com

Books published by Capstone Press are manufactured with paper
containing at least 10 percent post-consumer waste.

Library of Congress Cataloging-in-Publication Data
Saunders-Smith, Gail.
    Clouds / by Gail Saunders-Smith.
        p. cm.
    Includes bibliographical references and index.
    Summary: Describes different kinds of clouds—cirrus, cumulus, stratus, and
nimbus—and the types of weather they indicate.
    ISBN-13: 978-1-56065-777-4 (hardcover)
    ISBN-10: 1-56065-777-4 (hardcover)
    ISBN-13: 978-0-7368-4918-0 (softcover pbk.)
    ISBN-10: 0-7368-4918-1 (softcover pbk.)
    1. Clouds—Juvenile literature. [1. Clouds.] I. Title.
    QC921.35.S28   1998
    551.57'6—dc21   98-5051
                                                            CIP
                                                            AC

Note to Parents and Teachers

This book describes and illustrates many kinds of clouds and the type of weather they
indicate. The close picture-text matches support early readers in understanding the text.
The text offers subtle challenges with compound and complex sentence structures. This
book also introduces early readers to expository and content-specific vocabulary. The
expository vocabulary is defined in the Words to Know section. Early readers may need
assistance in reading some of these words. Readers also may need assistance in using the
Table of Contents, Words to Know, Read More, Internet Sites, and Index/Word List
sections of the book.

Printed in the United States of America in North Mankato, Minnesota.
092014   008431R

Table of Contents

Clouds form when warm air rises and cools. Clouds are made of very small water drops. The drops stick to dust in the air.

Clouds bring rain and snow. Rain falls when the air is above the freezing temperature. Snow falls when the air is below the freezing temperature.

Clouds come in many shapes. Meteorologists study cloud shapes. A meteorologist is a person who studies the weather. The shapes of the clouds tell meteorologists what kind of weather is coming.

Cirrus clouds form high in the sky. They are very thin. People can see through cirrus clouds. Cirrus clouds mean that we will have good weather.

Cumulus clouds have flat bottoms and puffy tops. Small, white cumulus clouds mean good weather. Big, dark cumulus clouds bring thunder and heavy rain.

Stratus clouds are gray and flat. They cover most of the sky. They form low in the sky. Light snow or drizzle sometimes falls from stratus clouds. Drizzle is a light rain.

Nimbostratus clouds are like stratus clouds. They are flat and cover most of the sky. But they are dark gray. They form higher in the sky. Nimbostratus clouds bring rain or snow.

Fog is a cloud, too. Fog happens when a cloud forms close to the ground. Fog goes away when the water drops dry up. Wind and heat can make fog dry up.

Clouds carry rain and snow.
Wind pushes clouds across
the sky. Clouds carry water
to places all over the world.

Words to Know

cirrus—thin clouds that form high in the sky

cumulus—clouds with flat bottoms and high, puffy tops

drizzle—a light rain

dust—tiny pieces of dirt that gather in the air

freezing—very cold; the point at which water turns to ice, which is 32 degrees Fahrenheit (0 degrees Celsius)

meteorologist—a person who studies the weather

nimbostratus—flat, dark gray couds that cover most of the sky; nimbostratus clouds are like stratus clouds, but they form higher in the sky.

stratus—flat, gray clouds that cover most of the sky

temperature—the measure of how hot or cold something is

Read More

Fowler, Allan. *What Do You See in a Cloud?* Rookie Read-About Science. New York: Children's Press, 1996.

Merk, Ann and Jim. *Clouds.* Weather Report. Vero Beach, Fl.: Rourke Corp., 1994.

Supraner, Robyn. *I Can Read about Weather.* Mahwah, N.J.: Troll, 1997.

Internet Sites

FactHound offers a safe, fun way to find Internet sites related to this book.

Go to *www.facthound.com*

FactHound will fetch the best sites for you!

Index/Word List

Word Count: 249
Early-Intervention Level: 20

Editorial Credits
Lois Wallentine, editor; Timothy Halldin, design; Michelle L. Norstad, photo research

Photo Credits
Brian A. Vikander, 12
Cheryl A. Ertlet, 1, 16
Cheryl R. Richter, 4, 14, 20
PictureSmith/Larry Mishkar, cover
Root Resources/John Kohont, 6, 18; Louise K. Broman, 10
Unicorn Stock Photos/Jim Shippee, 8